Disney
LEARNING

English Grammar

From the movie
Disney
FROZEN

AGES
6-7

KEY STAGE 1

SCHOLASTIC

Scholastic Children's Books
Euston House,
24 Eversholt Street,
London NW1 1DB, UK

A division of Scholastic Ltd
London ~ New York ~ Toronto ~ Sydney ~ Auckland
Mexico City ~ New Delhi ~ Hong Kong

This book was first published in Australia in 2014 by Scholastic Australia.
Published in the UK by Scholastic Ltd, 2015

ISBN 978 1 4071 6285 0

Printed in United Kingdom by Bell and Bain Ltd, Glasgow

6 8 10 9 7 5

Welcome to the Disney Learning Programme!

Children learn best when they are having fun! The **Disney Learning Workbooks** are an engaging way for your child to explore language along with fun characters from the wonderful world of Disney.

The **Disney Learning Workbooks** are carefully levelled to present new challenges to developing learners. Designed to support the National Curriculum for English at Key Stage 1, they offer your child the opportunity to practise skills learned at school and to consolidate their learning in a relaxed home setting with support from you. With interactive stickers, games, puzzles, flash cards and mini books your child will have fun learning punctuation and grammar!

The book contains exercises on sentence structure, parts of speech, tenses and punctuation. There are clear instructions and useful guidelines to support your child's writing.

Throughout the book you will also find 'Let's Read' stories featuring characters from the Disney movie **_Frozen_** for you to enjoy sharing with your child. Reading for pleasure and enjoying books together is a fundamental part of learning. Keep sessions fun and short. Your child may wish to work independently on some of the activities or you may enjoy doing them together – either way is fine.

Have fun with the Disney Learning programme!

Developed in conjunction with Catherine Baker, Educational Consultant

Let's Learn Grammar

In this book, you will learn about the rules we all follow when writing. You can practise when to use capital letters, full stops and more.

Don't forget to follow these rules:

- Use a capital letter at the beginning of every sentence.

Winter is cold.

- Use a capital letter for the names of people and places.

Anna   Elsa   Arendelle

- Use a capital letter when you write the word I.

When do I go?

Check your writing for the correct punctuation.

- Use a full stop at the end of a statement.

Olaf likes the summertime.

- Use a question mark at the end of a question.

Where is Elsa?

- Use an exclamation mark at the end of an exclamation.

Sisters are the best!

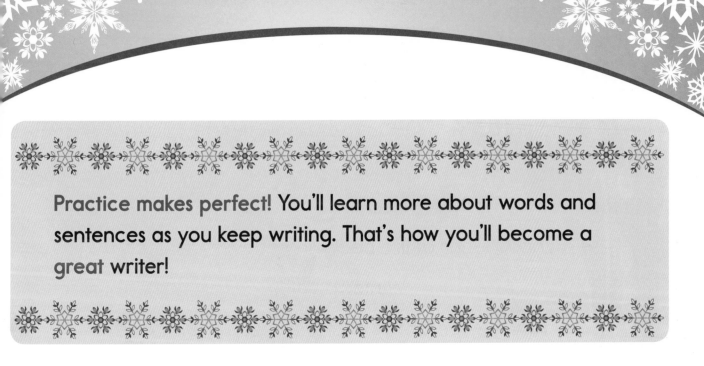

Practice makes perfect! You'll learn more about words and sentences as you keep writing. That's how you'll become a great writer!

Watch your endings.

- Add an **s** to the end of nouns if you are talking about more than one.

  one snowflake   two snowflakes

- Add an **s** to verbs that tell what one person, animal or thing does.

  The girl walks.

- Add **s** or **ed** to verbs that describe something now or in the past.

  Today, Anna laughs.

  Yesterday, Anna laughed.

Let's Read

It is a snowy day in Arendelle. Anna and Kristoff are in the mountains. The air is very cold, so they have both dressed very warmly. Sven the reindeer has come with them.

They walk below some snowy trees. The leaves have fallen off the trees. The bare branches are hanging down with long drops of ice. They look like crystals!

'Oh!' cries Anna. 'It's so beautiful!'

Kristoff nods his head. Even he is impressed!

They hear a voice behind them and turn around. There is a snowman standing under the trees.

'Hi!' he says. 'My name is Olaf. I like warm hugs.'

Anna and Kristoff are amazed. Not only does this snowman talk, he likes warm things!

Let's Learn About Sentences

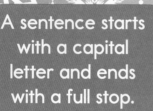

A sentence starts with a capital letter and ends with a full stop.

Draw a line under each sentence.
The first one is done for you.

warm hugs

<u>Olaf likes warm hugs.</u>

Sven and Kristoff are good friends.

good friends

This is a snowman.

snowman

is blowing

The wind is blowing.

Let's Learn About Word Order

Find and match the stickers.
Draw a line under the sentence that shows
the words in the correct order.

1. She hugs the snowman.

   The snowman hugs she.

2. The book writes she in.

   She writes in the book.

3. He kisses her hand.

   Hand her he kisses.

4. Her tea sips she.

   She sips her tea.

Let's Learn About Capital Letters

A sentence begins with a capital letter.

Write the correct word to complete each sentence.
The first one is done for you.

1. __The__ queen is happy.

the
The

2. __She__ smiles.

She
she

3. __It__ is a sunny day.

It
it

4. __Will__ she go outside to play?

will
Will

Let's Learn About the Subject of a Sentence

The **subject** of a sentence is the person or thing doing the action. Draw a line under the **subject** of each sentence. The first one has been done for you.

1. The wind is blowing.

   is blowing

   The wind

2. The snow is white.

   is white

   The snow

3. Anna and Elsa play in the snow.

   play in the snow

   Anna and Elsa

4. They make snowballs.

   They

   make snowballs

11

Let's Learn About the Object of a Sentence

If the **subject** is doing something to someone or something, that someone or something becomes the **object** of the sentence. Draw a line under the **object** of each sentence. The first one has been done for you.

1. Kristoff sees some carrots.

   Kristoff

   <u>some carrots</u>

2. Elsa goes to the mountain.

   ~~the mountain~~

   Elsa

3. Olaf loves the summer.

   <u>the summer</u>

   Olaf

4. Anna sees some snow.

   Anna

   <u>some snow</u>

Let's Make Sentences

Draw a line to match the **subject** and
the **object** in the sentences below.
The first one has been done for you.

subject	object
Sven	buys a treat.
Kristoff	uses magic.
Elsa	sings pretty songs.
Anna	loves carrots.

Let's Write Sentences

Use the words from the box to write a **subject** or an **object** to complete each sentence.

Anna   her   They

_____

- -
(subject)
_____ falls over.

_____

- -
Hans helps _____ (object)
_____ up.

_____

- - - - - - - - - - - - - - - - - - - -
(subject)
_____ smile at each other.

Let's Write Sentences

Draw your favourite character or use one of the stickers from the sticker sheet. Write two sentences about the picture. Use words from the box if you need to.

snow   trees   waterfall   white
cold   frosty   fun

Let's Punctuate

Check each sentence for capital letters
and correct punctuation.

Remember to use a
capital letter at the
beginning of every
sentence. Don't forget
the punctuation mark
at the end.

the moon comes out at night

it is big and round

it is shining brightly

Write the story with the correct punctuation here.

Let's Make Sentences

Cut out the puzzle pieces on pages 17 and 19. Match the puzzle pieces to make sentences.

Cut out the puzzle pieces on pages 17 and 19.

Be careful of sharp scissors. Ask an adult to help.

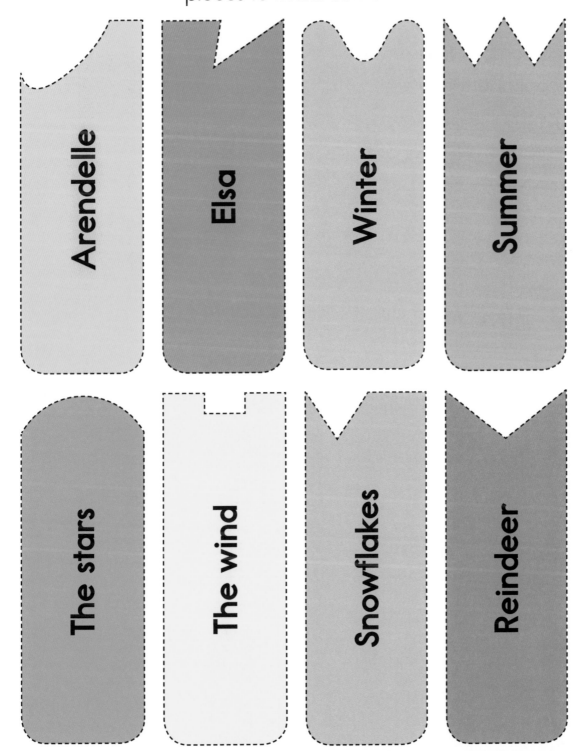

Arendelle

Elsa

Winter

Summer

The stars

The wind

Snowflakes

Reindeer

Let's Make Sentences

blows strongly.

fall on the ground.

is the queen.

is a kingdom.

is warm.

love carrots.

is cold.

shine in the sky.

A **statement** is a sentence that tells you something.

A **statement** begins with a capital letter and ends with a full stop. Draw a line under each statement.

1.

Who is clapping?

The lady is clapping.

2.

This is a cottage.

this is a cottage

3.

Is the bird flying?

The bird is flying.

4.

Elsa makes it snow.

Who makes it snow?

Let's Learn About Questions

A question is a sentence that asks something.

A **question** begins with a capital letter and ends with a question mark. Use the words in the box to complete each question.

| Who | What | Where | When |

1. _____ is riding the sleigh?

2. _____ are they going?

3. _____ will they do?

Let's Write
Statements and Questions

Use the words in the box to write a statement.
Then write a question.

dances	Anna	is
who	she	smiling
at	him	with

Write a statement. Remember to begin with a capital letter.

_____

- -

_____

- -

_____

Write a question. Don't forget to add a question mark at the end.

_____

- -

_____

_____

- -

Let's Learn About Exclamations

An **exclamation** begins with a capital letter and ends with an exclamation mark. Draw a line under the exclamations.

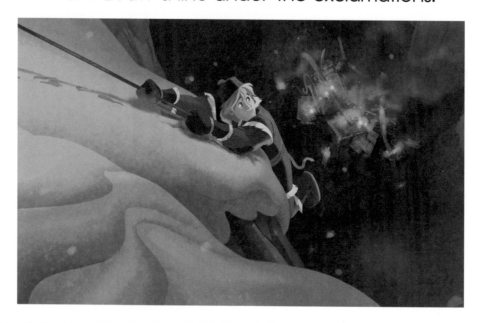

Watch out, Kristoff!

Kristoff hangs on.

There goes the sleigh!

The sleigh is on fire.

Will Kristoff fall?

Look at the wolves!

Let's Write
Different Sentences

Write sentences about Elsa.

1. What statement can you tell Elsa?

sace

sose

2. What question can you ask Elsa?

3. What exclamation can you write about Elsa?

Let's Sort Sentences

Write each sentence in the correct box below.

Can she catch a snowflake?

Anna is cold!

How does Elsa do that?

Elsa is making it snow!

Anna watches Elsa.

Snowflakes fall down.

Statements

Questions

Exclamations

Let's Write Questions

Questions end with a question mark.

Draw someone in this picture or use one of the stickers from the sticker sheet. Write two questions about the picture. Use words from the box to help.

Who	**What**	**When**
Why	**Where**	**How**

_____

- -

_____

- -

_____

- -

_____

Let's Write a Story

Use the words to write a story containing
a statement, question and exclamation.

Remember to use a
capital letter at the
beginning of each
sentence and a full
stop, question mark
or exclamation mark
at the end.

Anna woke up

is she still sleepy

what a messy room

Write the story with the correct punctuation here.

Let's Write Sentences

Write a question that Anna would ask Kristoff.
Then write a statement that Kristoff says to Anna.
Remember to use the correct punctuation.

Let's Learn About Nouns

A noun is the name of a person, place or thing.

Find and match the stickers.
Draw a line under the **noun** that names each picture.
The first one has been done for you.

<u>ship</u>

car

shop

castle

glove

shoe

candle

vase

cow

horse

window

door

Let's Write Nouns

Write the correct noun to complete each sentence.

castle	hand	Hans	flowers

1. Here is _____ .

2. He is holding Anna's _____ .

3. There are _____ everywhere.

4. They are outside the _____ .

Let's Sort Nouns

Find and match the stickers. Write each noun in the correct column. More than one noun can go in each column. Can you think of any other nouns?

town   pencil   mountain

window   sister   Hans

Person	Place	Thing
Olaf	castle	sleigh

page 52

© Disney

© Disney

Snow Queen
© Disney

© Disney

ELSA
© Disney

Anna
© Disney

DISNEY
FROZEN
© Disney

Let's Explore Plurals

Adding **-s** to nouns makes them **plural**. Find and match the stickers. Draw a line under the noun that names each picture. Are they single or plural? Tick the correct box.

soldier

soldiers

Single ✓   **Plural**

mitten

mittens

Single   **Plural**

queen

queens

Single   **Plural**

carrot

carrots

Single   **Plural**

boot

boots

Single   **Plural**

bucket

buckets

Single   **Plural**

Let's Write Plurals

Write the plural for each noun.

1. flower

2. bee

3. dandelion

4. frying pan

5. lantern

Let's Learn About Proper Nouns

Proper nouns begin with a capital letter.
Draw a line under the proper nouns below. Write the names correctly.
The first one has been done for you.

1. olaf loves summertime.

$\qquad$ Olaf

2. He tells anna all about it.

3. What will kristoff say?

4. sven does not say anything.

Write a sentence about what your friend likes to do.
Remember to use a capital letter for your friend's name
and end the sentence with a full stop.

_____   _____

likes to   _____

Proper nouns are also used for the names of places.

Draw a line under the proper nouns below.
Write the places correctly. The first one has been done for you.

1. <u>arendelle</u> is a cold country.

Arendelle

2. It is not hot like africa.

3. The north mountain is cold as well.

Write the name of the place where you live.
Remember to use a capital letter.

I live in _____ .

Let's Write with Proper Nouns

Look at the chart. Choose a person's name.
Then choose a place. Use the words to write a statement.

People names	Place names
Elsa	**Arendelle**
Anna	**The North Mountain**
Hans	

Let's Punctuate

Check each sentence for capital letters and correct punctuation.

Remember to use a capital letter at the beginning of every sentence and for proper nouns (name of a person or place).

where does anna live

she lives in arendelle

it is very cold there

Write the story with the correct punctuation here.

Let's Write

Read these sentences about Elsa.

Elsa is elegant.

Elsa is lovely.

Elsa is sweet.

Elsa is amazing.

Now write sentences about Anna in the same way.
Remember to begin with a capital letter and end with a full stop.

a

n

n

a

'I would love to feel the warm sun on my face,' says Olaf. 'I would love to spend a day on the beach on the hottest day of summer. I have always liked the idea of summer!'

Anna and Kristoff look at each other. They know what happens to cold things when they get warm. Olaf will melt!

'I am going to tell him,' whispers Kristoff.

'Don't you dare!' says Anna. 'After all, even a snowman deserves to have a dream!'

Let's Learn About Verbs

Verbs are called 'doing' words.

Find the stickers.

Draw a line under the **verb** that describes the action in each picture.

ride

walk

write

dance

yawn

smile

sit

stand

skate

swim

smile

yell

Let's Write Verbs

Write the correct verb to complete each sentence.

| smiles | holds | skates | laughs |

1. Anna _____.

2. Elsa _____ Anna's hand.

3. She _____ at her sister.

4. Anna _____.

Let's Add *-s* to Verbs

To say what one person (he or she) is doing, add the suffix *–s* to the verb.

Choose the correct verb to complete each sentence.

1. Anna ____________________ for Elsa.

look
looks

2. Anna ____________________ her sister.

love
loves

3. She ____________________ Anna.

hug
hugs

4. She ____________________ her sister.

protect
protects

Let's Add -*ed* to Verbs

Add the suffix -*ed* to verbs to show that something happened in the past.

Draw a circle around the suffix **-ed** in the sentences below.

1.  We rolled snowballs.

2.  We picked the flowers.

3.  We danced at the ball.

4.  We looked at the paintings.

Let's Learn About
am, is and *are*

Am, is and *are* tell us about now, or the present. Use *am* when you talk about I. Use *is* when you talk about a thing or person. Use *are* when you talk about more than one thing or person.

Write **am, is** or **are** to complete each sentence.

_____

1. I _____ writing.

_____

2. Anna _____ on a horse.

_____

3. She _____ singing.

_____

4. The horses _____ going to the mountain.

Write a sentence using the verb **am.**

_____

_____

Let's Learn About
was and *were*

Write **was** or **were** to complete each sentence.

> **Was** and **were** tell us about the past. Use **was** when you talk about one thing or person. Use **were** when you talk about more than one thing or person.

_____

1. Elsa _____ very happy.

_____

2. Snowflakes _____ flying everywhere.

_____

3. The wind _____ blowing.

_____

4. The trees _____ swaying.

Write a sentence using the word **was**.

_____

Let's Write About
the Present and the Past

Use the verbs below to write a sentence that tells you about **the present**. Then use the verbs to write a sentence that tells you about **the past**.

jump

knock

play

_____

- -

_____

- -

_____

_____

- -

_____

- -

_____

Draw a ⭕ around the verb that tells about the present.

Draw a ▢ around the verb that tells about the past.

Silly Sentences

This is a game for two or more players

Be careful of sharp scissors. Ask an adult to help.

Set Up

- Cut along the dotted lines. Make a pile of pink noun cards and a pile of blue verb cards. Mix up each pile and place them face down.
- Give each player a pencil and paper.
- Decide which player will go first.

How to Play Silly Sentences

- Turn over one verb card and one noun card. Each player writes down a silly sentence using the words on the cards. For example, if *clap* and *kitchen* were turned over, one possible silly sentence could be, *I can clap my toes together in the kitchen.*
- Players take turns reading their silly sentences out loud.
- Play continues until all the cards have been used.

Noun Cards

snowman	castle
tree	kitchen
game	mountain
trolls	bedroom
sister	queen

Verb Cards

jumped	cooked
laughs	eats
sing	played
talks	throw
clap	hides

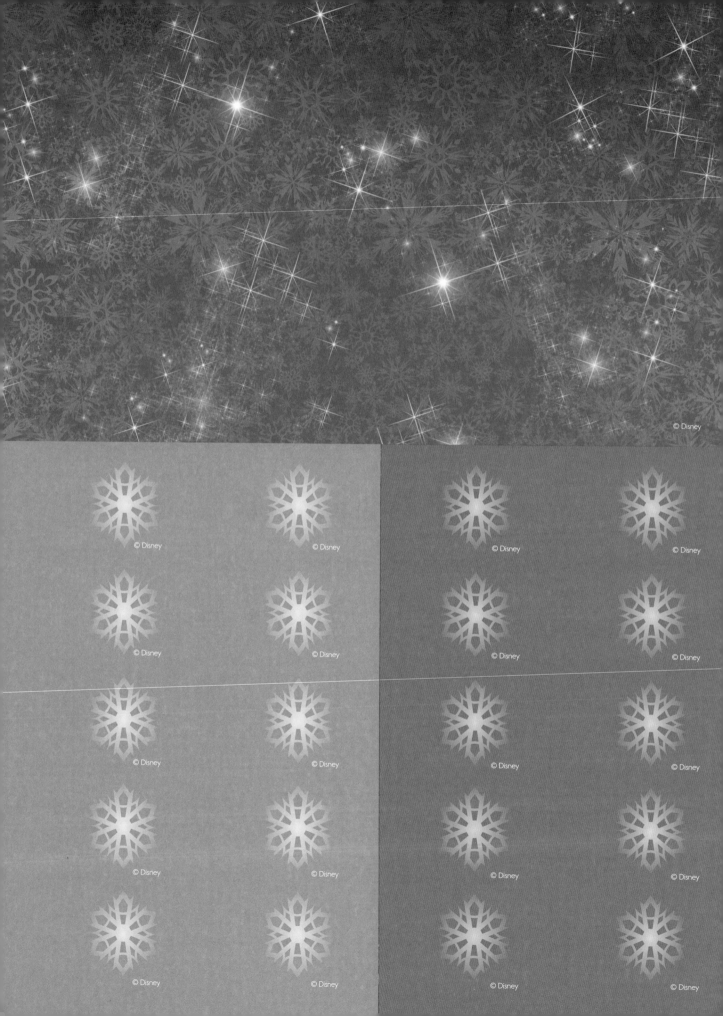

Let's Write a Story

Read the story.
Check each sentence for capital letters, correct
spelling and punctuation.

Remember to use
the correct verb
for the past and the
present. Check that
you've used a capital
letter for any proper
nouns (names of
people or places).

kristoff climb the mountain

he find lots of ice

he tooks it down the mountain.

Write the story with the correct punctuation here.

Let's Learn About Adjectives

An adjective is a 'describing word'.

An adjective gives more information about a noun (a person, place or thing). Find and match the stickers. Draw a line from each adjective to the noun it is describing.

1. cold

2. green

3. big

4. blue

Let's Sort Adjectives

Adjectives can tell us more about a noun, such as its size, number or colour. Sort each adjective into the correct column.

| big | blue | one | white | ten | tiny |
| four | little | red | green | two | huge |

Size	Number	Colour

Let's Write Adjectives

Write the correct adjective to complete each sentence.

cold   big   three   blue

1. Elsa wears a _____ dress.

2. Olaf has _____ buttons.

3. Anna feels a _____ wind.

4. Kristoff has a _____ sleigh.

Let's Add -er to Adjectives

Write the correct adjective.
The first one has been done for you.

1. A bright lantern.   This lantern is **brighter** .

2. A big bird.   This bird is _____ .

3. Some long stairs.   These stairs are _____ .

4. Fast wolves.   This sleigh is _____ .

Let's Add -est to Adjectives

Write the correct adjective.
Use **-er** and **-est**. The first one has been done for you.

Add the suffix **-est** to an adjective to describe how three or more things are different.

1. big **bigger** **biggest**

2. long

3. dark

4. small

Let's Write Adjectives

Write the correct adjective to complete each sentence.

soft	tall	two	long

1. Sven stood under a _____ tree.

2. There were _____ drops of ice.

3. Sven's _____ antlers were tangled.

4. Kristoff looked at the _____ snow.

Let's Use Nouns, Verbs and Adjectives

Choose a suitable adjective,
noun and verb to fill in the gaps.

Remember adjectives
are 'describing words'.
Nouns are the names
of people, places
or things. Verbs are
'doing' words.

It is adjective **in winter.**

We can have fun in the noun **.**

Do you like to verb **in the snow?**

Write the story here.

Let's Write Adjectives

Use four of these adjectives to write a silly story.
Read your story to a friend.

purple	funny	tall	round
tiny	stinky	sad	red

1. The _____ snowman was happy.

2. He could see _____ children.

3. They lived in _____ houses.

4. They played _____ games.

Now use four new adjectives
to tell another silly story!

Let's Sort Nouns, Verbs and Adjectives

Read the words. Write each word in the correct column.
Write one more word in each column.

three	looks	hair
pond	sleep	boat
long	blue	jumped

Nouns	Verbs	Adjectives

Let's Review

Read the sentences. Draw a ◯ around each noun.
Draw a ☐ around each adjective. Underline each verb.

Olaf dances in the green meadow.

The hot sun shines brightly.

A fuzzy bee buzzes around.

Big flowers grow everywhere!

What will Olaf do in the meadow?

Let's Review

Read the sentences. Draw a ◯ around each verb.
Draw a line under each statement in BLUE.
Draw a line under each question in RED.
Draw a △ around each exclamation mark.

Look at this mess!

Who made this mess?

Anna and Elsa tidy up the floor.

They put their toys away.

How do you help to clean up at home?

I _____

Queen Elsa is delighted to meet Olaf. Suddenly, he starts to melt under the hot sun! Anna gasps.

'Here you go, little guy,' says Elsa. Using her magic powers, she creates a snow cloud above Olaf's head. Anna claps her hands in delight. Olaf will never melt now!

Olaf is very excited by his snow cloud.

'Now I can go to the beach!' he cries.

'The beach is lots of fun,' says Elsa. 'But you know what else is fun? Ice-skating!' She waves her hand and turns the castle's Great Hall into ice.

Kristoff and Anna run and put on their ice skates. Sven tries to skate with them, but he is very clumsy! His hooves slide around in every direction. Kristoff has to help him stand up straight.

Olaf is having fun with his new friends. What a perfect way to end the day!

Answers

Let's Learn About Sentences

Draw a line under each sentence.
The first one is done for you.

warm hugs

Olaf likes warm hugs.

Sven and Kristoff are good friends.

good friends

This is a snowman.

snowman

is blowing

The wind is blowing.

8

Let's Learn About Word Order

Find and match the stickers.
Draw a line under the sentence that shows
the words in the correct order.

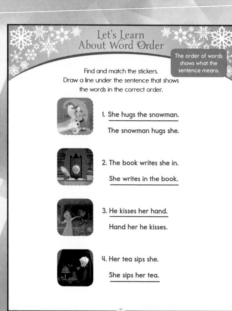

1. **She hugs the snowman.**
   The snowman hugs she.

2. The book writes she in.
   She writes in the book.

3. **He kisses her hand.**
   Hand her he kisses.

4. Her tea sips she.
   She sips her tea.

9

Let's Learn About Capital Letters

Write the correct word to complete each sentence.
The first one is done for you.

1. **The** _____ queen is happy.   the / The

2. **She** _____ smiles.   She / she

3. **It** _____ is a sunny day.   It / it

4. **Will** _____ she go outside to play?   will / Will

10

Let's Learn About the Subject of a Sentence

The subject of a sentence is the person or thing
doing the action. Draw a line under the **subject** of
each sentence. The first one has been done for you.

1. The wind is blowing.   is blowing / **The wind**

2. The snow is white.   is white / **The snow**

3. Anna and Elsa play in the snow.   play in the snow / **Anna and Elsa**

4. They make snowballs.   **They** / make snowballs

11

Let's Learn About the Object of a Sentence

If the subject is doing something to
someone or something, that someone or something becomes
the object of the sentence. Draw a line under the **object** of
each sentence. The first one has been done for you.

1. Kristoff sees some carrots.   Kristoff / **some carrots**

2. Elsa goes to the mountain.   **the mountain** / Elsa

3. Olaf loves the summer.   **the summer** / Olaf

4. Anna sees some snow.   Anna / **some snow**

12

Let's Make Sentences

Draw a line to match the subject and the object
in the sentences below.

subject	object
Sven	buys a treat.
Kristoff	uses magic.
Elsa	sings pretty songs.
Anna	loves carrots.

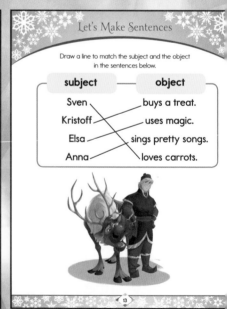

13

66

Answers

Let's Write Sentences

Use the words from the box to write a **subject** or an **object** to complete each sentence.

Anna	her	They

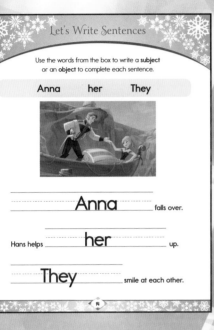

_____ **Anna** _____ falls over.

Hans helps _____ **her** _____ up.

They _____ smile at each other.

Let's Write Sentences

Draw your favourite character or use one of the stickers from the sticker sheet. Write two sentences about the picture. Use words from the word box if you need to.

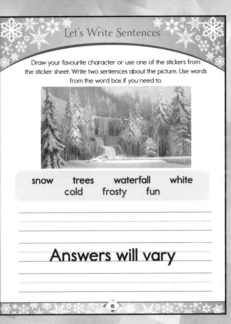

snow	trees	waterfall	white
cold	frosty	fun	

_____

Answers will vary

_____

Let's Punctuate

Check each sentence for capital letters and correct punctuation.

Remember to use a capital letter at the beginning of every sentence. Don't forget the punctuation mark at the end of every sentence.

the moon comes out at night

it is big and round

it is shining brightly

Write the story with the correct punctuation here.

The moon comes out at night. It is big and round. It is shining brightly.

Let's Make Sentences

Cut out the puzzle pieces on pages 17 and 19. Match the puzzle pieces to make sentences.

Be careful of sharp scissors. Ask an adult to help.

Arendelle	is a kingdom.
Elsa	is the queen.
Winter	is cold.
Summer	is warm.

Let's Make Sentences

The stars	shine in the sky.
The wind	blows strongly.
Snowflakes	fall on the ground.
Reindeer	love carrots.

Let's Learn About Statements

A statement is a sentence that tells you something.

A **statement** begins with a capital letter and ends with a full stop. Draw a line under each statement.

1. 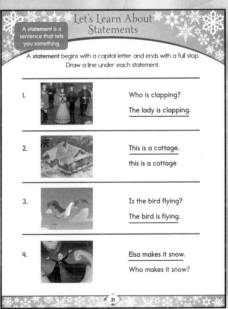 Who is clapping?
   The lady is clapping.

2. This is a cottage.
   this is a cottage

3. Is the bird flying?
   The bird is flying.

4. Elsa makes it snow.
   Who makes it snow?

Answers

Let's Learn About Questions

A question is a sentence that asks something.

A **question** begins with a capital letter and ends with a question mark. Use the words in the box to complete each question.

Who	What	Where	When

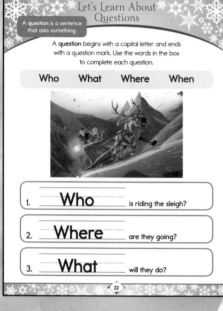

1. **Who** is riding the sleigh?
2. **Where** are they going?
3. **What** will they do?

Let's Write Statements and Questions

Use the words in the box to write a statement. Then write a question.

dances	Anna	is
who	she	smiling
at	him	with

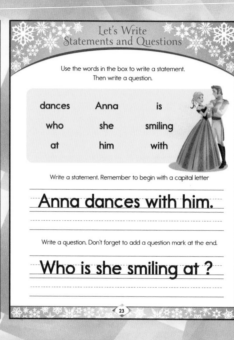

Write a statement. Remember to begin with a capital letter

Anna dances with him.

Write a question. Don't forget to add a question mark at the end.

Who is she smiling at ?

Let's Learn About Exclamations

An exclamation is a sentence that shows surprise or strong feelings.

An **exclamation** begins with a capital letter and ends with an exclamation mark. Draw a line under the exclamations.

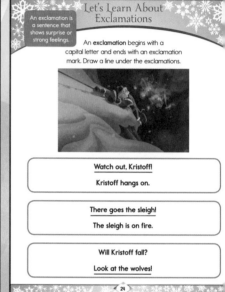

Watch out, Kristoff!
Kristoff hangs on.

There goes the sleigh!
The sleigh is on fire.

Will Kristoff fall?
Look at the wolves!

Let's Write Different Sentences

Write sentences about Elsa.

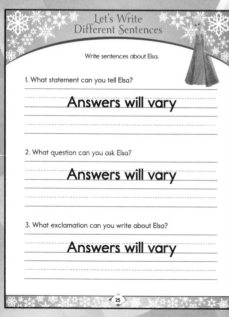

1. What statement can you tell Elsa?

Answers will vary

2. What question can you ask Elsa?

Answers will vary

3. What exclamation can you write about Elsa?

Answers will vary

Let's Sort Sentences

Write each sentence in the correct box below.

Can she catch a snowflake?
Anna is cold!
How does Elsa do that?

Elsa is making it snow!
Anna watches Elsa.
Snowflakes fall down.

Statements

Anna watches Elsa.
Snowflakes fall down.

Questions

Can she catch a snowflake?
How does Elsa do that?

Exclamations

Anna is cold!
Elsa is making it snow!

Let's Write Questions

Questions end with a question mark

Draw someone in this picture or use one of the stickers from the sticker sheet. Write two questions about the picture. Use words from the box to help.

Who	What	When
Why	Where	How

Answers will vary

Answers

Let's Write a Story

Use the words to write a story containing a statement, question and exclamation.

Remember to use a capital letter at the beginning of each sentence and a full stop, question mark or exclamation mark at the end.

Anna woke up

is she still sleepy

what a messy room

Write the story with the correct punctuation here.

Anna woke up.

Is she still sleepy?

What a messy room!

28

Let's Learn About Nouns

A noun is the name of a person, place or thing.

Find and match the stickers.
Draw a line under the **noun** that names each picture.
The first one has been done for you.

ship	shop
<u>ship</u>	shop
car	<u>castle</u>

| glove | <u>candle</u> |
| shoe | vase |

| cow | window |
| <u>horse</u> | door |

30

Let's Write Nouns

Write the correct noun to complete each sentence.

| castle | hand | Hans | flowers |

1. Here is **Hans** .

2. He is holding Anna's **hand** .

3. There are **flowers** everywhere.

4. They are outside the **castle** .

31

Let's Sort Nouns

Find and match the stickers. Write each noun in the correct column. More than one noun can go in each column. Can you think of any other nouns?

| town | pencil | mountain |
| window | sister | Hans |

Person	Place	Thing
Olaf	castle	sleigh
Hans	**mountain**	**window**
sister	**town**	**pencil**

32

Let's Explore Plurals

A plural means more than one.

Adding **–s** to nouns makes them **plural**. Find and match the stickers. Draw a line under the noun that names each picture. Are they single or plural? Tick the correct box.

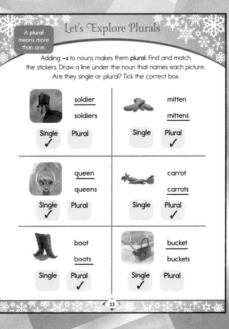

soldier	mitten
<u>soldiers</u>	<u>mittens</u>
Single ✓ Plural	Single Plural ✓

<u>queen</u>	carrot
queens	<u>carrots</u>
Single ✓ Plural	Single Plural ✓

boot	bucket
<u>boots</u>	<u>buckets</u>
Single Plural ✓	Single ✓ Plural

33

Let's Write Plurals

Write the plural for each noun.

1. flower **flowers**

2. bee **bees**

3. dandelion **dandelions**

4. frying pan **frying pans**

5. lantern **lanterns**

34

69

Answers

Let's Learn About Proper Nouns

Proper nouns are used for the names of people.

Proper nouns begin with a capital letter.
Draw a line under the proper nouns below. Write the names correctly.
The first one has been done for you.

1. olaf loves summertime.　　**Olaf**

2. He tells anna all about it.　　**Anna**

3. What will kristoff say?　　**Kristoff**

4. sven does not say anything.　　**Sven**

Write a sentence about what your friend likes to do.
Remember to use a capital letter for your friend's name
and end the sentence with a full stop.

Answers will vary

_____ likes to _____ .

35

Let's Learn More About Proper Nouns

Proper nouns are also used for the names of places.

Draw a line under the proper nouns below.
Write the places correctly. The first one has been done for you.

1. arendelle is a cold country.

Arendelle

2. It is not hot like africa.

Africa

3. The north mountain is cold as well.

North Mountain

Write the name of the place where you live.
Remember to use a capital letter.

I live in　**Answers will vary**　.

36

Let's Write with Proper Nouns

Look at the chart. Choose a person's name.
Then choose a place. Use the words to write a statement.

People names	Place names
Elsa	**Arendelle**
Anna　Hans	**The North Mountain**

Answers will vary

37

Let's Punctuate

Check each sentence for capital letters
and correct punctuation.

Remember to use a capital letter at the beginning of every sentence and for proper nouns (name of a person or place).

where does anna live

she lives in arendelle

it is very cold there

Write the story with the correct punctuation here.

Where does Anna live?

She lives in Arendelle.

It is very cold there.

38

Let's Write

Read these sentences about Elsa.

Elsa is elegant.

Elsa is lovely.

Elsa is sweet.

Elsa is amazing.

Now write sentences about Anna in the same way.
Remember to begin with a capital letter and end with a full stop.

Answers will vary

a

n

n

a

39

Let's Learn About Verbs

Verbs are called 'doing' words.

Find the stickers.
Draw a line under the **verb** that describes the action in each picture.

ride / **walk**	**write** / dance
yawn / smile	sit / **stand**
skate / swim	**smile** / yell

42

70

Answers

Let's Write Verbs

Write the correct verb to complete each sentence.

| smiles | holds | skates | laughs |

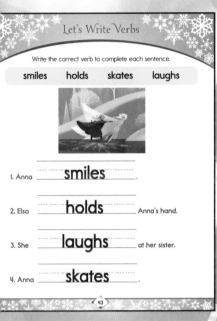

1. Anna __smiles__.

2. Elsa __holds__ Anna's hand.

3. She __laughs__ at her sister.

4. Anna __skates__.

43

Let's Add -s to Verbs

To say what one person (he or she) is doing add the suffix -s to the verb.

Choose the correct verb to complete each sentence.

1. Anna __looks__ for Elsa.
   - look
   - looks

2. Anna __loves__ her sister.
   - love
   - loves

3. She __hugs__ Anna.
   - hug
   - hugs

4. She __protects__ her sister.
   - protect
   - protects

44

Let's Add -ed to Verbs

Add the suffix -ed to verbs to show that something happened in the past.

Draw a circle around the suffix -ed in the sentences below.

1. We roll(ed) snowballs.

2. We pick(ed) the flowers.

3. We danc(ed) at the ball.

4. We look(ed) at the paintings.

45

Let's Learn About am, is and are

Am, is and are tell us about now, or the present. Use am when you talk about I. Use is when you talk about a thing or person. Use are when you talk about more than one thing or person.

Write am, is or are to complete each sentence.

1. I __am__ writing.

2. Anna __is__ on a horse.

3. She __is__ singing.

4. The horses __are__ going to the mountain.

Write a sentence using the verb am.

__Answers will vary__

46

Let's Learn About was and were

Was and were tell us about the past. Use was when you talk about one thing or person. Use were when you talk about more than one thing or person.

Write was or were to complete each sentence.

1. Elsa __was__ very happy.

2. Snowflakes __were__ flying everywhere.

3. The wind __was__ blowing.

4. The trees __were__ swaying.

Write a sentence using the word was.

__Answers will vary__

47

Let's Write About the Present and the Past

Use the verbs below to write a sentence that tells you about **the present**. Then use the verbs to write a sentence that tells you about **the past**.

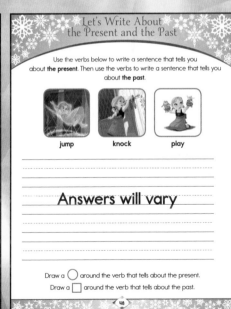

jump   knock   play

__Answers will vary__

Draw a ◯ around the verb that tells about the present.
Draw a ▢ around the verb that tells about the past.

48

Answers

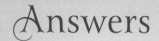

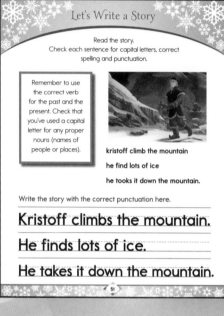

Let's Write a Story

Read the story.
Check each sentence for capital letters, correct spelling and punctuation.

Remember to use the correct verb for the past and the present. Check that you've used a capital letter for any proper nouns (names of people or places).

kristoff climb the mountain

he find lots of ice

he tooks it down the mountain.

Write the story with the correct punctuation here.

Kristoff climbs the mountain.

He finds lots of ice.

He takes it down the mountain.

51

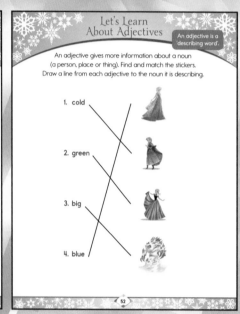

Let's Learn About Adjectives

An adjective is a 'describing word'.

An adjective gives more information about a noun (a person, place or thing). Find and match the stickers. Draw a line from each adjective to the noun it is describing.

1. cold

2. green

3. big

4. blue

52

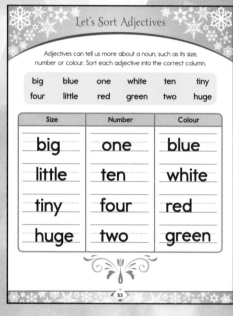

Let's Sort Adjectives

Adjectives can tell us more about a noun, such as its size, number or colour. Sort each adjective into the correct column.

| big | blue | one | white | ten | tiny |
| four | little | red | green | two | huge |

Size	Number	Colour
big	one	blue
little	ten	white
tiny	four	red
huge	two	green

53

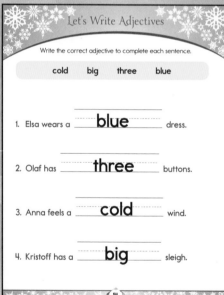

Let's Write Adjectives

Write the correct adjective to complete each sentence.

| cold | big | three | blue |

1. Elsa wears a **blue** dress.

2. Olaf has **three** buttons.

3. Anna feels a **cold** wind.

4. Kristoff has a **big** sleigh.

54

Let's Add -er to Adjectives

Add the suffix –er to an adjective to describe how two things are different.

Write the correct adjective.
The first one has been done for you.

1. A bright lantern. This lantern is **brighter**.

2. A big bird. This bird is **bigger**.

3. Some long stairs. These stairs are **longer**.

4. Fast wolves. This sleigh is **faster**.

55

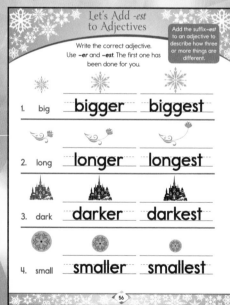

Let's Add -est to Adjectives

Add the suffix –est to an adjective to describe how three or more things are different.

Write the correct adjective.
Use –er and –est. The first one has been done for you.

1. big **bigger** **biggest**

2. long **longer** **longest**

3. dark **darker** **darkest**

4. small **smaller** **smallest**

56

Answers

Let's Write Adjectives

Write the correct adjective to complete each sentence.

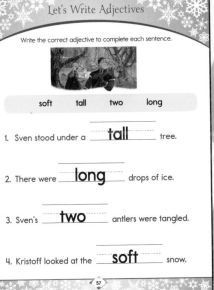

| soft | tall | two | long |

1. Sven stood under a **tall** tree.

2. There were **long** drops of ice.

3. Sven's **two** antlers were tangled.

4. Kristoff looked at the **soft** snow.

57

Let's Use Adjectives Nouns and Verbs

Choose a suitable adjective, noun and verb to fill in the gaps.

Remember adjectives are 'describing words'. Nouns are the names of people, places or things. Verbs are 'doing' words.

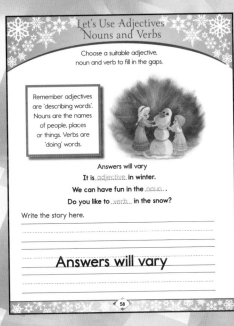

Answers will vary
It is _adjective_ in winter.
We can have fun in the _noun_.
Do you like to _verb_ in the snow?

Write the story here.

Answers will vary

58

Let's Write Adjectives

Use four of these adjectives to write a silly story.
Read your story to a friend.

| purple | funny | tall | round |
| tiny | stinky | sad | red |

1. The _____ snowman was happy.

Answers will vary

2. He could see _____ children.

3. They lived in _____ houses.

4. They played _____ games.

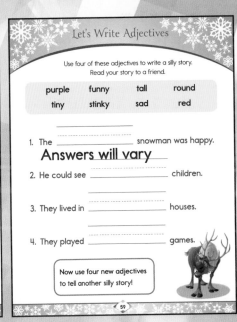

Now use four new adjectives to tell another silly story!

59

Let's Sort Nouns, Verbs and Adjectives

Read the words. Write each word in the correct column.
Write one more word in each column.

three	looks	hair
pond	sleep	boat
long	blue	jumped

Nouns	Verbs	Adjectives
pond	looks	three
hair	sleep	long
boat	jumped	blue

60

Let's Review

Read the sentences. Draw a ◯ around each noun.
Draw a ☐ around each adjective. Underline each verb.

(Olaf) dances in the [green] meadow.

The [hot] (sun) shines brightly.

A [fuzzy] (bee) buzzes around.

[Big] (flowers) grow everywhere!

What will (Olaf) do in the (meadow)?

61

Let's Review

Read the sentences. Draw a ◯ around each verb.
Draw a line under each statement in ▬▬▬.
Draw a line under each question in ▬▬▬.
Draw a △ around each exclamation mark.

(Look) at this mess △

Who (made) this mess?

Anna and Elsa (tidy) up the floor.

They (put) their toys away.

How do you help to clean up at home?

I **Answers will vary**

62

Here Are All
the Things I Can Do

I can ...

Identify and order parts of a sentence ◯

Identify **nouns** ◯

Identify the **subject** of a sentence ◯

Add the suffix **–s** to nouns to make plurals ◯

Identify the **object** of a sentence ◯

Add the suffix **–s** to verbs to describe what one person does ◯

Write a statement ◯

Write **proper nouns** for people and places ◯

Write a question ◯

Use a capital letter to begin **proper nouns** ◯

Write an exclamation ◯

Identify **verbs** ◯

Use a capital letter to begin a sentence ◯

Add **–s** to some verbs to describe what is happening now ◯

Use full stops, question marks and exclamation marks correctly ◯

Add **–ed** to some verbs to describe what happened in the past ◯

I can ...

Put a snowflake sticker next to the things that you can do!

Use **am**, **is** and **are**

Use **was** and **were**

Identify **adjectives**

Add **–er** and **–est** to compare nouns

More Activities to Share with Your Child

How does your child learn?

Research shows that children benefit from a wide range of learning activities. Here are a few exercises you can do together to strengthen your child's understanding of punctuation and grammar.

Hunt for punctuation marks

Give your child one to two minutes to look through a page from a newspaper or magazine. Ask them to circle different kinds of punctuation marks, such as full stops, question marks and exclamation marks. Read the sentences together to help your child recognise how your voice changes when you read statements, questions and exclamations.

Make word mats

Take three A4 sheets of cardboard, and write NOUNS on the first sheet, VERBS on the second and ADJECTIVES on the third. Give your child a collection of old magazines to look for colourful pictures. Ask them to find pictures of people, places and things to design the NOUNS mat. Find pictures of actions words for the VERBS mat, and pictures of describing words for the ADJECTIVES mat. Together, think of interesting ways to label the pictures with coloured pens and pencils and other craft materials. Laminate or use clear sticky back plastic to cover the completed mats.

Expand sentences with adjectives

Write a noun on a piece of paper, such as *car*. Ask you child to add more words that describe that noun. Add one word at a time. For example: car; small car; small yellow car; small yellow shiny car.

Storytelling fun

Give each family member or friend a piece of paper. Fold the paper into thirds, and ask each person to write an adjective on the front fold, a noun on the middle fold and a verb on the last fold. Then pass the paper to the next person, who repeats the process by adding a second word to each fold. Repeat the process until all the players have put a word on each fold. When the paper returns to the first person, you are ready to play. Take turns using the words to make silly sentences or tell stories.

Play word games

Find It: Display a long object, such as a ruler. Ask your child to find something longer. Then ask your child to find something that would be the longest of the three objects. Put the objects together to compare them. Repeat the game with tall, taller, tallest and small, smaller, smallest.

Concentration: Use index cards to create a set of word cards. Write the following words: boat, boats, friend, friends, bird, birds, sister, sisters, flower, flowers. Read and talk about the meaning of each word. Work with your child to make pictures for each of the words. Mix up the cards, and then place them in rows. Take turns trying to match the single and plural forms of each word. The player with the most card pairs wins the game.

Grammar Snap: Keep the following hand-clapping rhythm going as you think of verbs (doing words). Slap your thigh, then clap your hands, then snap your fingers (first with your right hand and then with your left). The rhythm sounds like this: slap, clap, snap, snap. The first player begins by saying, 'Doing words!' Then the players take turns naming verbs to the snapping beat.

For example:

Slap, clap, snap, **'run'**

Slap, clap, snap, **'hop'**

Slap, clap, snap, **'jump'**

Slap, clap, snap, **'walk'**

Repeat the activity with adjectives that describe people, places or things. The first player would begin by saying, 'Adjectives: people!' etc.

Make picture/word strings

Collect an assortment of pictures of your child's favourite foods – use photographs or pictures from magazines. Help your child clip the pictures onto a long piece of string with paper clips. Ask your child to write a word on an index card to describe each of the pictures. Encourage them to use words that describe how each food item tastes, smells or feels. Clip the words next to the pictures and see how many adjectives your child can clip onto the strings.

CONGRATULATIONS!

_____
(Name)

has completed the Disney Learning Workbook:

ENGLISH GRAMMAR

Presented on

_____
(Date)

_____
(Parent's Signature)